Building The Team

Raven Kaldera and Joshua Tenpenny

Building The Team

Cooperative Power Dynamic Relationships

Raven Kaldera
and Joshua Tenpenny

Alfred Press
Hubbardston, Massachusetts

Alfred Press
12 Simond Hill Road
Hubbardston, MA 01452

Building The Team: Cooperative Power Dynamic
Relationships
© 2013 by Raven Kaldera and Joshua Tenpenny
ISBN 978-0-9828794-6-7

Printed in cooperation with
Lulu Enterprises, Inc.
860 Aviation Parkway, Suite 300
Morrisville, NC 27560

*To Joshua, who helped develop this system,
to V-boy, who proved it worked on others,
to Dr. Bob Rubel who said that we should
write the book,
and for all the M/s folks who told us that it
transformed their relationships.*

Thank you,

and you're welcome.

Contents

Pre-Foreword

Robert (Dr. Bob) Rubel

Raven and Joshua saved our relationship. This book may very well save yours.

Let me explain.

Jen Crider is my partner. Actually, she's my Owner. But more important than the relationship structure, she and I have different strengths. Because of my Asperger Syndrome, order and routine are my friends and *thinking* is easier for me than *feeling*. In fact, many Aspies (including me) find the world of *feelings* to be baffling and confusing.

In my eight years as Master to a slave, I followed a mythical paramilitary/Leather Model of autocratic rule: governance by a single person having virtually unlimited power. My slave's role was to follow my directions, period. I was not interested in my slave's buy-in. I'm sure that my non-standard brain wiring helped to urge me down this path, but I also took this path because at that time, there was very little literature on how to approach Master/slave relationship structures. We were all making it up as best we could, and those who *knew* how to maintain long-term structured relationships weren't very open about sharing their knowledge.

And then Jen entered my life and she became my Leader. But Jen wasn't an autocratic-leader type, she was a Team-Player type of leader. That turned out to be a problem. As an Aspie, I hadn't been socialized to be a team player and not only did I not understand "team-player" rules, but those kinds of rules were foreign to the way I was used to living. Being twenty years older than Jen, I'd been living my own way for quite a while.

Like many Aspies, I live by rulebooks: this is the way I interact with person A, this is the way I interact with person B, this is... So I was something like a bucket of ice water thrown onto Jen's enthusiastic win-win model of management. I was lost; she was lost. I was upset; she was upset. We were doomed. We weren't speaking the same model of *relationship,* and we were so far apart conceptually that we couldn't tell *what* was wrong, only that what we were trying to do probably wouldn't work.

And then came Raven and Joshua. They saved us.

Because I don't speak "Team" and because Jen does, she is the person qualified to understand Raven's book and comment on it for other readers. So the "real" Foreword is hers, and rightfully so.

DR. ROBERT RUBEL
AUSTIN, TEXAS
JUNE, 2013

The Real Foreword

Jen Crider

Fairly soon after entering the world of BDSM, I became exposed to what I'll loosely call the "traditional version of Master/slave relationships". It was hard not to become aware of this version of M/s, as my partner, Robert J. (Dr. Bob) Rubel was already seriously well known within the community because of the number of books he'd written about this topic and the extensive conference presentations he was making about them. You might say that his very "way of being in the world" was saturated to overfilling with this point of view about structured relationships.

As my romance with Dr. Bob started to veer towards the power-exchange path, I realized that the traditional M/s structure that he had lived for eight years was not going to be the right path for our particular relationship. I was drawn to build a relationship where we were both working toward a common goal, where we would use our individual strengths to become a power couple, and where we would have hot sex every night. He was totally committed to the hot sex, but the "cooperative work towards a common goal" concept rather eluded him.

To be honest, we struggled. Despite attending many, many M/s conferences with Bob, I couldn't find anyone living in a Master/slave relationship who was living the model I wished to show him. Quite frankly, Bob (with Asperger Syndrome) couldn't make any sense of my style of leadership after all his years submerged in a more traditional Leather Master/slave relationship. Even more challenging – and almost incomprehensibly to me – he had no team-building experience. He is a researcher. His value comes from being able to make sense of widely differing points of view. There is nothing about Bob that has ever had anything to do with teams or teamwork.

I was frustrated, and Bob grew Wary of the Unknown. I began to suspect that this was not going to turn out well.

The turning point came for us after attending classes given by Raven and Joshua at "Leather" and Master/slave conferences. For me, this occurred during South Plains Leatherfest in March of 2012. Finally, I had found someone who was describing the way I wanted to structure my Total Power Exchange (TPE) relationship. For Bob, the turning point came six months later while attending the Master/slave Conference in Washington, DC in September 2012. He attended the same class I had attended six months before, and got to hear Raven and Joshua clearly explain what I had been saying for a year and a half. Miraculously, it seemed to me, he was now on-board and understood the direction I wished to take the relationship. He named what we were doing a "CEO/COO" model because he understood those roles due to his years working in the corporate world for a female CEO.

In November 2012 we attended a weekend intensive given by Raven and Joshua at Castle Griffin in Maryland. There, we were immersed for two days in the details and background concepts that support the theories of his "Teamwork Model"; and we learned how power-imbalanced adversarial relationships don't support the Teamwork Model, even though both management styles involve senior and junior partners. Ultimately, we came to appreciate what Raven stresses in this book: relationships succeed because of what we *do* rather than what we *feel*.

You will learn in this book and in their classes that it is critical for slave to embrace the *spirit* of Master's law rather than become distracted by the *letter* of Master's law. In this book and in their classes, Raven explains that the spirit of Master's law must eventually permeate the slave's mindset so that Master's point-of-view simply becomes *the way things are done*. This turned out to be a lesson that we could use.

Within days of returning from Raven and Joshua's long and intense weekend of study and introspection at Castle Griffin, I implemented Raven's idea of a "puppet master" that Joshua had initially written about in his book *Real Service,* and that they had again discussed during the weekend classes. Ultimately, this saved our relationship. Within weeks of returning to Austin, Bob began to filter his actions through the "Jen" puppet that he could visualize sitting on his shoulder when I was not near him. To my personal surprise (edging up on Astonishment) this enabled him to think, "What would Jen want me to do in this situation?"

And it worked. Practically overnight. Sonofabitch!

So here you are, about to start reading Raven's latest book. Bob and I hope that you enjoy it … but frankly we have no doubt that you're going to enjoy it, for if you've waded through this much of the Foreword, you're clearly a committed M/s-geek.

So I'll stop writing and let you get on with reading. This book encourages M/s pairs to decide for themselves how to use their particular dynamic as an exoskeleton – something that can protect them as they experience difficult times – and all relationships experience difficult times. To help keep you and your partner focused, Raven has placed study questions at the ends of chapters.

Specifically, these questions are meant to help the two of you to strengthen the dynamics of your relationship.

Personally, the path that Bob and I have trod has not been easy – and it remains a work in progress. We were not as lucky as you: we didn't have this book to guide us. If you are just starting your M/s journey, or if you are searching for a fresh approach to M/s to revitalize your M/s relationship, Bob and I are confident that you will find that Raven's Teamwork Model will give you plenty to think about. This book – like all Raven's books – is written in a conversational style: it feels as though they're speaking with you, their friends, on a topic that deeply interests both of you.

Oh, in case it isn't obvious by now, Bob and I encourage you to attend as many "Raven and Joshua" classes you can, read their books, and learn from watching them interact. These men are bringing fresh ideas to a budding group of new Masters and slaves, and bringing clarity and thoughtfulness to a field previously left to improvisation within the context of autocratic rule. These men are thinking outside the box of "traditional" structured relationships as practiced in the BDSM culture as we know it today.

Jen Crider
Dr. Bob's Owner
Austin, Texas
June, 2013

Part 1: Teamwork

Why We Call This A Team

We've been together in a power dynamic relationship – meaning a consenting relationship of negotiated inequality, sometimes referred to as "master/slave" or "dominant/submissive" – for eleven years now. For the last several years, we've also been counseling new D/s and M/s couples when they have obstacles in their relationships, and we've found that many of them give up quickly because they try to follow a model that doesn't work for them ... and it's the only model they can find.

We call this model, the one that is most commonly spread throughout BDSM fiction and even much of the nonfiction, the model of *adversarial* relationships. We'll discuss, shortly, why we are using that term, but suffice it to say that it puts the master and slave in opposing positions, and the master "acts on" or "does to" the slave in an ongoing dance of disobedience and punishment. There are a lot of people who love this sort of dynamic, but there seem to be an equal number (if not more) for whom it just doesn't work. When they try it and fail, they often tend to give up on M/s entirely, which makes us sad. We aren't trying to wipe out the adversarial dynamic; we're trying to provide an alternative, which we call the Teamwork model. After years of counseling couples (and triples, and more) who are failing badly with adversarial M/s, we can honestly say that there's a need for alternatives, as quickly as possible.

The alternative that we've worked out can be adapted to any level of intensity of power dynamic, from a part-time limited dynamic of dominance and submission all the way to a total-power-exchange internal-enslavement piece of property who has given up all their recourse. It doesn't matter how much control the two of you agree that one will have over the other; you can still be partners on a Team. And lest the words "partners" and "Team" seem too egalitarian for you, remember that in business, there are senior partners and junior partners – and a good Team has a team captain. In our dynamic, Raven is the senior partner and Joshua the junior partner, but they are both partners in the work of making the relationship function. Raven is the Team captain, but we are still on the same Team.

When we began teaching about this model of master/slave relationships, some people – usually women in romantic heterosexual relationships which had grown out of or replaced their vanilla marriage – were put off by what they considered to be a "corporate" model of how to be together. "I don't want to feel like he's the boss and I'm just an employee," we heard as a common complaint. However, we are stressing in this book that our model can work for any type of master/slave relationship, from the most formal and service-only to the most romantic of long-term unequal marriages.

It's possible that our language may seem a bit "corporate" – which is hilarious as Raven has never worked in a corporate career, although Joshua has – but it's mostly because we are two fairly intellectual men with a strong working partnership. While we do love each other very much, we tend to see this relationship in terms of what we do rather than what we feel, and we both tend to approach problems from an analytical standpoint rather than an emotional one. Keep in mind that Teamwork doesn't have to be distant; the mental metaphor can also be reminiscent of a pair of skilled ballroom dancers. One is leading and the other is following, but the ideal is that both are mindful and aware of the others' movement in order to waltz smoothly and gracefully around the room. People see them and say in wonder, "I don't know how they do it! Why, it's like they're two parts of one being. It's so beautiful." And there's little that's more romantic than that, in our eyes anyway.

Some definitional notes: Throughout this book we'll be switching genders, using *he*, *she*, and sometimes *they* as a singular ungendered pronoun (as in "...someone's at the door and they want to talk to you..."). However, we will be using the word "master" for the person on the top side of the dynamic, regardless of gender, because this is the way it tends to be used in our M/s community, by both men and women. We would like to make it clear, once and for all, that we believe completely in gender equality, and that people of every gender find success and happiness in all of these roles.

We will also be using the word "slave" for the person on the bottom side, even if they do not identify as such (and even though we are not thrilled with the word "slave"; on the other hand we can't come up with anything better). The terms "dominant" and "submissive" are perfectly serviceable, and many people find them to be a better descriptor of their relationships than the disputed and baggage-laden "master" and "slave", but for the moment the D/s words are also used to refer to personal qualities as much as relational roles, and we're talking about roles in this book, not how someone thinks of themselves. Some people also use the words "master" and "slave" to refer to personal qualities regardless of the existence of any relationship, but we think of them as relational, and they are used more in that vein than the D/s titles. So we're going with them.

We'll also make liberal use of the word "couple", but don't think we're assuming that all masters and slaves are monogamous, or only paired with a single person. We are polyamorous ourselves, and we know the joys and difficulties of balancing multiple relationships. However, learning to be a Team starts with the relationship between two people, and when they've got it working reasonably well, others can get on the same Team. This means that a master with two slaves, for example, should work separately on this with each of them before trying to integrate everyone all together.

At the end of each section of this book is a series of questions for the two of you to fill out. We strongly encourage you both to answer the questions separately, with no discussion beforehand, and then compare notes. You might be surprised at what the other person comes up with. If you're both right on the same page, great; but even if you aren't it's useful information with which to reassess your problem areas.

And one final note: When we say "we" in this book, we're referring to the two of us – Raven and Joshua. When you see an "I" in the ordinary text, it means Raven, who was the primary author of this text. In this book, Joshua is only speaking in the first person in specifically indicated quotes, although he has contributed extensively to its theory and practice.

Please keep in mind as you read this book that we aren't perfect yet ourselves at this complex dance. Sometimes we stumble, sometimes we're less than graceful, sometimes we even have to stop the music and go over the steps again with painful slowness.

Even so, when we're on our game and working together like a well-oiled machine, it's amazing to both of us. We never thought, in the beginning, that it would be this good. We promise you that it's possible, and we encourage you to find the time to practice this dance yourselves.

The Problem of Porn

Don't get us wrong, we love pornography. In fact, we've written pornography, and even had it published – but we don't forget the fact that it's fiction. In porn, masters and slaves never clash over who gets to eat the last box of lo mein takeout. In porn, mistakes are punished even if they were unavoidable, it's assumed that masters will be petty, and no one ever has a three-hour relationship processing session that involves talking rather than a sound beating. In porn, the master can tell the slave to like something, and eventually they will come to enjoy it (often in less than ten pages) for no reason other than the master's say-so. It's really not useful to base an everyday, real life on jack-off material, because genitals have a short attention span and tend to vacate the premises when there's hard work to be done.

However, most people will not have any models other than fiction on which to base their power dynamic relationship. They'll look at the porn masters and slaves and believe that this is how it works. There will be no other option for them to consider. That's why we think it's important to have other models, especially ones that lend themselves well to real life.

The Teamwork model that we explain here is not sexy. Talking about it does not make for exciting mental scenes. In fact, it is the opposite of fetishy – it's simply practical. But since relationships that are based mostly on sex don't tend to wear well from day to day, if you're actually trying to make a full-time power dynamic work, you're going to want something that can be used when there are no sexual sparks and the two of you have come to an impasse.

Porn is fun, but sooner or later the garbage needs to be taken out.

And now, to say one good thing about porn as it pertains to M/s relationships, because a porn-author friend asked me to. Eroticized behaviors of the sort found in pornography are good for creating heat in existing M/s relationships that are functioning well, but the master and slave are focusing on other things – perhaps even worthy things – that distract them from the spark and color that an erotic relationship can provide. Of course, not all M/s relationships are sexual and we understand that. However, for those that involve both sex and 24/7 real life, it sometimes happens that real life floods everything and drowns out the heat in a wash of kids and in-laws and angry bosses and unfair landlords and money troubles and health issues and dirty catboxes. In these cases, an infusion of porn can help you to remember why you got into this in the first place. Just use it as a vitamin pill, not the main meal, and you'll be fine.

Part 2: Non-Adversarial Relationships

Adversarial Relationships

When we first started giving workshops on non-adversarial relationships, some people were unhappy with that terminology. We need to make it very clear that by calling them adversarial, we are not judging them negatively. It's simply descriptive – and after months of tossing around other potential terms, we still can't come up with anything more accurate than adversarial. (Joshua points out that the term can be viewed more like having a sparring partner than an enemy.) In these relationships, it's not uncommon for the master and slave to be in opposing positions, often struggling with each other. We define adversarial power dynamics in this way:

+ The slave is passive and is worked on by the master, rather than working with the master. Taking an active role is discouraged. When the slave is not passive they are generally struggling against the master or the master's orders.

+ Disobedience is common ("...no one can be expected to be obedient all day, every day!"), and punishment is assumed to be an ongoing part of the relationship. Fear of punishment may be a primary motivation of the slave, especially in the beginning.

+ The slave is routinely "forced" to do things they are unwilling to do, and their initial unwillingness is not seen as a serious problem so long as they obey.

+ The master sets themselves apart from the slave, and says, in essence, *I am here and you are there, and I will make you do what I want.* There is an assumption that making the M/s work is a matter of force on the part of the master; the slave has little to no responsibility for whether or not the dynamic functions well as a whole.

✦ The slave's obedience is seen largely as a product of the master's training; the master generally gets full credit for it. The slave is, at best, good raw material.

We'd also like to make it clear that some D/s and M/s couples enjoy and do better in adversarial relationships, and would find the alternative immensely boring, or perhaps completely ineffective. We've spoken with couples who prefer this style and do well with it, and we've found that it can be a much more useful style for the following types of individuals:

✦ **Masters and slaves who eroticize the adversarial moments, and find the "takedown" hot or emotionally satisfying.** While we've said repeatedly that you can't base a full-time live-in power dynamic relationship primarily around sex (because the genitals have such a short attention span), it does play a strong role in more of our relationships, and to rob the dynamic of that which gives it the most spark can make it unsatisfying. Folks who have the adversarial relationship as their fetish often say things like, "If my slave was always obedient, I'd be bored!" and "I test my master all the time because I love to know where the end of my leash is." They feel that the difficulties of negotiating day-to-day disputes in an adversarial relationship are well worth it, and they find the continual conflicts are worth the thrill – and the conflict itself, especially if it ends with a takedown, can be the main part of the thrill.

✦ **Slaves who don't want adult responsibilities**. If a slave's primary motivation for entering into a power dynamic is to take refuge from all responsibility and decision-making, including for their own behavior, they are unlikely to find the Teamwork model satisfying. This may especially be true if the slave has a lot of personal or professional responsibilities in their life outside of the relationship, and they want a space where they can let all of that go.

✦ **Slaves who are only marginally more submissive than their masters.** These are usually situations where two dominant people get into a relationship, and rather than hashing out some sort of egalitarian compromise, the more dominant of the two manages to take complete control of the relationship.

✦ **Slaves with impulse control problems.** While many slaves would be offended at the idea that they would go into a power dynamic because they lacked self-control and needed someone else to supply it, we've talked to a surprisingly high number of slaves who have admitted to just that. Some of them cited years of impulsive bad decisions that left their lives in shreds, and that turning those lives over to a more sensible and disciplined person was the best thing they ever did for themselves. Many of these slaves don't consider themselves to be particularly submissive as people, and the combination of a lack of intrinsic submission and poor self-control means that they continually act out and require adversarial slapdowns. Whatever their feelings about the conflict in the moment, they all agreed that they were better off this way.

✦ **Slaves who have trouble letting go of authority and control.** Some slaves *want* to be able to obey smoothly, at least in theory, but when it comes time to let go of authority, they can't make themselves submit. They lash out and grab for whatever control they can get, sometimes in a panicked response to years of outside conditioning. Some of these slaves have been in very dominant positions in other areas of their life, or came from a background where they have felt they had to continually grab for control in order to feel safe. Those reactions can take years or even decades to outgrow, and in the meantime they felt safer with a guarantee of fast, brutal retaliation as soon as they step out of line.

✦ **Slaves who are currently suffering from a mental illness which prevents them from fully participating in a Teamwork situation.** This can be temporary or a long-term situation. While the specifics of handling a slave with an active mental illness are beyond the scope of this book (see our forthcoming book *Broken Toys: Submissives With Mental Illness And Neurological Disorders*), suffice it to say that some masters have managed to keep their slave on track through such difficult times, but the methods tend to be adversarial when the slave is no longer able to control themselves well enough to be consistently obedient. (It is also expected that the master would be getting them any other mental health help they might need during this time.)

We're going to put in yet another disclaimer here, before you go any further. From this point on, when we say that a particular behavior isn't going to work, we mean that *it won't work in the Teamwork model.* It may work with other styles of relationship, but that's not relevant to this book. Please remember this as you continue reading.

The Teamwork Model

In contrast, the Teamwork model is characterized by these qualities:

✦ The basic premise is that the slave wants to obey, and eventually to achieve an excellent standard of obedience. The master wants this as well.

✦ Intentional disobedience is very rare, and is a sign that there are serious fundamental issues with the relationship.

✦ Fear is never a motivation for the slave. The best motivations are achievement, excellence in their role, wanting the relationship to go well, and wanting to please the master.

✦ The assumption of both parties is that the responsibility for making the M/s dynamic work is equally on both people. Each member of the Team has to do their part.

✦ The slave is not a passive recipient, but actively and openly colludes with the master to bring about the goals of the relationship.

✦ Problems are handled not with blame and punishment, but with mutual brainstorming and implementation of solutions.

People who might do better with the Teamwork model than the Adversarial model:

✦ **People with childhood abuse trauma, or serious parent issues.** That includes both masters and slaves with abuse histories. Adversarial relationships can trigger panic or negative feelings, on either side of the slash. Slaves can blindly rebel because it reminds them of the traumatic situation, and masters may be uncomfortable at hearing themselves act, even distantly, like the people who hurt them.

✦ **Working partnerships.** Some slaves are unpaid (or even sometimes actually paid) employees for their master's business. When the master is boss as well as domestic captain, it makes much more sense to do things in a more businesslike manner.

✦ **Partnerships where the slave has a great deal of real-world responsibility.** Some slaves practically run the entire household so that their master can sit back and concentrate on their own work, secure in knowing that the bills will get paid, the children fed, and the floor cleaned. In these relationships, both parties are keeping track of a great number of details – and working together smoothly is crucial to the well-being of the household, which may contain other people. It's necessary for the slave to embrace motivations that propel them toward real obedience, and it's in the master's best interest to support that ideal.

✦ **Manipulative slaves.** Since the Teamwork model rests on the slave understanding and following the spirit of the law rather than its letter, a manipulative loophole-finding slave can be headed off by these methods. We are assuming that both parties in this endeavor are essentially willing to be honest with each other; if the slave is a chronic liar or pathological manipulator or has a personality disorder, that's a bigger problem. However, some slaves are lawyerly types who are used to manipulating the rules in order to get what they want, which is a very adversarial position to be in. We'll deal with that problem next.

The Spirit Of The Law

The Teamwork model relies entirely on the slave understanding the spirit of each rule rather than scrutinizing the letter of the master's law, usually in order to find loopholes and justify unwanted behavior. The slaves who are most likely to do this are usually intelligent, highly verbal people who enjoy arguing and can do it for hours on end. The intelligent master will avoid the whole argument and ask them about the spirit of the law they violated: *Do you really believe that if you'd asked me, this would have been what I'd told you I wanted you to do?* It's the question that silences the whole loophole argument, assuming that the slave in question is even trying to be honest. Usually that question is followed by a pause and a mumbled "Well … no." The follow-up, of course, is to ask "What do you think I'd have wanted you to do?" and "So, knowing that, why did you make the choice you made?"

Sometimes, of course, the slave will answer that first crucial question in the affirmative. When that happens, one of two things are probably going on: either they're lying (which requires backing the whole relationship up to the remedial stage), or the master did an insufficient job of explaining their worldview to the slave who is supposed to be aligning themselves with it. Masters, being imperfect, will occasionally assume that the slave will just pick it up from watching them. It's true that a good slave *will* be watching their master constantly, but observations can be subject to a lot of misinterpretation. It's better to actively help build that inner world, so as to make sure that it's an accurate reflection of the master's own paradigm.

The ideal, in essence, is for a slave to have a little "master puppet" in their head who resembles their actual master, and not the ideal master they've secretly fantasized about for decades. In fact, one of the biggest hurdles that a new master may have is the process of hunting down, murdering, and replacing that original master puppet with one who wears their own visage. The internal master puppet, when asked, will deliver an accurate version of what the slave should be doing in any situation. One slave described it as having an invisible letter bracelet inscribed with "WWMW" – What Would Master Want?

This kind of solid knowledge, thorough enough to be extrapolated to new situations with reasonable accuracy, is only achieved by the master actively teaching the slave about their inner mental world, their values, their expectations, and especially their priorities. One useful technique is to periodically ask the slave, "What do you think I'd want in this situation?" This question can describe a theoretical state of affairs, or the decision that the master is facing in the moment.

If the slave doesn't know – and they should be encouraged to be honest about their ignorance, and not ridiculed for getting the answer wrong – then it is up to the master to teach them. ("No, that's not what I'd do, and here's why, and here's what I believe that supports that decision. I'd do this instead. Can you figure out why?") After months or years of this quizzing, there can be no argumentative excuse about what the master would want. The spirit of the law should eventually permeate the slave's mindset, until it becomes simply the way that things are done.

Of course, some masters are more predictable than others. If a master loves variety to the point where the "master puppet" could conceivably give any number of valid answers to the "What Would My Master Want In This Situation", the slave needs to have a good understanding regarding which subjects they will have no reliable way of knowing the current preferences about. In these cases, the goal is for them to know how their master prefers them to handle this. When should they stop until they have clarification? When should they just make their best guess without bothering their master? When should they have a back-up plan in case they've guessed wrong? The point of this is not to railroad the master into being rigid or predictable, but to create a base of knowledge and structure to help the slave constantly know what is expected of them.

Bringing It Back Around, Again And Again

Ideally, it's the job of both people in the relationship to remind each other about the Teamwork agreement when they find themselves facing off with a "me vs. you" attitude. In reality, however, the responsibility is weighted toward the master. If the slave forgets, the master can bring them back to it, but if the master forgets it can be difficult for the slave to remind them of the agreement without sounding disrespectful or manipulative. This means that there's more consequence laid on the master, by definition. In our relationship, it is primarily my job to bring myself up short when I start becoming adversarial, and it's also my job to remind my slaveboy, again and again, that *we are a Team, we are in this together, we can find a way through the mess if we work as a Team.*

It's also my job to remind him that we chose to be an inegalitarian Team for a reason, and that we have both discovered the hard way that the Team always functions better when I'm in charge. (This works much better when there are years of track record behind you to point at, so be patient and verbally mark the times when that point is made particularly clear.) Don't let the word "team" come to denote "equality", because it doesn't have to. If everyone on the Team agrees that everything goes better when Team Captain gets their way, then everyone can be committed to making that happen. (Similarly, don't let the terms "partners" throw you off by seeming too egalitarian when we use them.

Sometimes, however, it's the master who gets stuck and forgets about Teamwork. While the slave has no ability to force the master to do anything, an intelligent master will give their slave leave to remind them when they forget. Of course, the slave can be trained to give the reminder in a way that the master doesn't see as argumentative; that process is described in the Modification chapter.

The Blame Game

Slaves have a tendency to want to lay blame when something goes wrong, either on themselves or someone else. However, when it comes to Teamwork, assigning fault is not the main point. The problem may well be caused by the behavior of one person, or it may be a problem created by both people together, or even by someone or something outside of the relationship, but blaming creates an adversarial situation. Instead, both parties should first focus on possible things that can be done – by either or both – to fix the problem and make sure that it does not happen in the future. In addition, some slaves use blame as a way to separate themselves from the situation: "It wasn't my fault that this happened, so I shouldn't have to be the one to fix it." Rather than "You screwed up, so it's your fault and you have to do X next time," it should be "The Team is going to solve this, and first this Team member is going to do X next time, and the other Team member is going to encourage and possibly remind them of it, and together we'll get through this."

It may be difficult for both people to move away from a blame model to a no-blame model, but it seems to be particularly difficult for slaves. Masters often adapt fairly quickly to a no-blame model when they see how well it works at getting through crises, but it may take a while before a slave learns to forgo blame. A no-blame model is also excellent for slaves who tend to fall into self-flagellation at any error. The master can just cut them off and say, "It doesn't matter whose fault it was. We just need to figure out why it happened, and then *we* need to figure out what *we* are going to do so that it doesn't happen again." Reward the slave with positive attention for being able to abort their self-loathing wallow and move quickly into problem-solving mode.

(For those people on both sides of the slash who are reading this and thinking, "But no blame means that the other person can get away with bad behavior!" please be reassured that this does not mean that responsibility will be shirked. Part of taking responsibility for an error, on the part of either party, is figuring out how to keep it from ever happening again, which is a step further down the line that we'll be covering soon. No one "gets away with" anything, because it is expected that an effort will be made toward improvement, and that's where all the energy should go. It should go without saying that if the master continually makes the same damaging errors and does not take any action to change the situation, there is something bigger going on that needs to be addressed.)

The first step – figuring out what went wrong – has to be handled with firmness, because it can easily fall back into self-flagellation for the slave or recriminations for the master. Keep voices level and focus on neutrally figuring out exactly where things went wrong. Giving the slave voice protocols – very formal ways of speaking when explaining what they did – can help distract from overwhelming emotions. So can using forced body language – you can make them sit erect rather than slouching, breathe regularly, hold their hands open and palm-up, relax their mouth and jaw, look you in the eye or focus on some comforting neutral point. The masters can use these techniques on themselves – just breathing, relaxing your tight jaw and softening your mouth, and opening your hands can help you to move into a problem-solving rather than a blaming space.

As soon as you figure out what went wrong, move straight into brainstorming. Any suggestion the slave comes up with is a good thing, and they should be complimented if they can come up with several possible ones. The master will be the one to decide which one sounds like it has the greatest chance of success, but it should be stressed to the slave that the more input they give, the more effective the final solution is likely to be. (Once a course of action has been reached, we find it useful to write it down immediately so that we don't forget exactly what we decided to do. Writing it down can also make it more "real" for us as a potential course of action rather than an exercise of playing with pie in the sky.)

Sometimes a course of action doesn't work, because the world is a flawed and imperfect place and that includes us. Both slaves and masters can be thrown into despair by this kind of failure, especially after they did all that work to come up with it. This usually means that they resort to draconian (and usually equally ineffective) measures, or give up entirely, letting resentment build up instead. The key to preventing this is to agree to a balanced level of investment. Both parties have to be just invested enough that they will actually follow through on the plan, but no more than that. They should keep enough emotional distance so that if it doesn't work out, they can go back to the drawing board as quickly as possible, without feeling crushed by disappointment or being tempted to fling recriminations. *It's an experiment, that's all. If it works, great. If it doesn't, we'll find another way.*

It's important to not only include the slave in the brainstorming process, but to make them feel like their input is desired and taken into account, if only so as to better manage their feelings in the matter. When the master lets the slave know that they are expected to help with problem-solving, the slave tends to be more committed to the outcome. Learning problem-solving skills may take time and practice, and the master may have to continually redirect the slave for a while. Even a useful question like "What could have been done to prevent this?" may send them into a tailspin of blame-seeking; it may behoove the master to make them rephrase the answer repeatedly until they can express it in a neutral format and tone. Keep in mind that being unwilling to participate in problem-solving may be a subconscious reluctance to change long-standing habits. Emphasize that you are both looking for a way to get the job done rather than an excuse to not do it.

Masters should keep an eye on how enthusiastically the slave engages in brainstorming with them. If the slave seems reluctant, has negative things to say about every possibility that the master comes up with, and doesn't have any good suggestions themselves, they may be consciously or unconsciously unwilling to create change in the situation. (They may also be unwilling to accept a Teamwork model; many slaves absolutely do not want to be expected to help solve problems.) It may be useful to take a recess of at least a day, and tell them to think about (or write down) why they are so reluctant even to think about ways to solve the problem. "I don't believe that it can be solved" is not a good answer. That's not their decision. It's the master's decision, and one hopes that the master has given the situation enough thought to be convinced that *something* can be done, if only some compensatory behavior or work-around.

Here we have to become philosophical for a moment, and talk about hope. In our opinions, a master who has given up hope is a sad and ineffective master. Just as it is the master's job to set the long-term goals, it is also their job to sustain hope in the achievement of those long-term goals, and to model that hope and belief for the slave to follow. If the goals do turn out to be less than achievable, the master's job is not to give up, but to choose alternate goals that actually are achievable. Actively making a different choice is not the same as losing hope and giving up; it's taking action in the face of new information. However, if the master slumps into hopelessness and apathy, the slave will generally follow, or at least go into a tailspin of panic.

Hope is also not the same thing as optimism. Optimism is a day-to-day attitude; hope is a long-term attitude. A master can be pessimistic on a daily basis yet still hold out hope for the long-term goals. (In fact, it's often the slave's job to provide short-term optimism, if they are any good at it.) Masters need to have a strong belief in their own goals, and the hope necessary to keep struggling in the face of difficulty. You'd be surprised how much a master's hope can buoy up a slave's heart when the storms are rising.

It took years to pull my slave away from the blame game. Every time something would go wrong, he would desperately try to affix blame, even when it seemed to get in the way of moving toward solutions. For a while, my exasperated response was just to take responsibility for everything: *It's all my fault. I'm the guy in charge, the buck stops here, so it's all my fault. Even if you did it. I should have figured out beforehand that you might do something stupid like that, and put a rule in place. It's a failure of knowing you well enough on my part. So now that we've established that, let's move on. What are we going to do about it?*

This approach did have the benefit of taking him aback enough to divert his blame-seeking behavior, since he was expecting me to attempt to avoid responsibility (that being his experience with most of the people in his life). Even if he thought that it actually was my fault, or that it was obviously his and I was being silly, it broke the chain of obsession and allowed me to move us on to the important part: *What are we going to do about it? And yes, I mean "we". Quit thinking about blame and start figuring out how we can prevent this in the future. We're a Team, and the Team made the mistake, and the Team is going to fix it.* Eventually that last part did sink in: blame was irrelevant, solution was everything, and we needed to engage the possibilities with joint enthusiasm.

In order to do this, however, we needed to move past the adversarial blame stage as quickly as possible, and ideally learn to skip it entirely. This took us years to get straight, and so if you find yourselves backtracking again and again to this one point, don't give up. Retraining one's self to plan instead of blame takes time, but we assure you it is possible.

One note to masters about using online forums as a place to extract possible ideas for conflict management: This can go well, or it can go very badly. First, please read extensively from the archives of that particular online list to make sure that it is an appropriate place to post such questions. Posting to the wrong place usually ends in mockery, or at the least a general lack of respect for your intelligence. Don't send your slave in to say, "My master wants me to ask what to do in this case." The forum members will probably assume that the master is "hiding behind the slave" or doesn't care enough about it to ask their own questions. For that matter, a better way would be to ask, "Has anyone ever been in this situation before? If so, what did you do that helped?"

Study Questions

1. Are there areas in your relationship where you've been doing things from an adversarial approach, and a Teamwork approach would work better?
2. Are there areas in your relationship where an adversarial approach works better (i.e. where the slave needs to be "forced")?
3. What obstacles do you face in maintaining a Teamwork approach?
4. Under what circumstances is it particularly difficult to remember to refocus each other on Teamwork?
5. What are ways in which you can overcome these obstacles? Brainstorm a few ideas.
6. What erotic fantasies and assumptions did you come to this relationship with? If they are too impractical for day-to-day life, what are more compartmentalized ways you can get those needs met? (For example, you might prioritize special "scene time" or "play" on a regular basis rather than expecting that hot story to be replayed on the day you're picking the kids up from a Little League game.)

Part 3:
Behavior
Modification

Modification Isn't Just A Tattoo

This model is, first and foremost, about behavior modification rather than punishment. While it is possible to use a punishment dynamic in a Teamwork model, the master needs to be very sure that the punishment is actually working to create better behavior. Ideally, it should slowly become obsolete as the slave gets into a more skillful groove and doesn't need it any more. Yes, really – in a M/s relationship where the behavior modification really works, punishment should eventually become a thing of the past. (That's assuming that you use punishment to begin with, which many people don't.)

The master should also be very alert for possible secondary gains when it comes to punishment. For those who haven't heard the jargon, secondary gains are side benefits from something that is otherwise unpleasant. In some cases, the side benefits are worth enough that they put up with and even seek out the unpleasantness. Some secondary gains around punishment might be:

+ **Getting attention.** For some people, even negative attention is better than no attention, and misbehaving can be a way of getting instant attention, even if it's active displeasure. Remember that attention rewards action. We have suggestions further on for ways to rob consequences of the attention factor.

+ **Getting a catharsis.** This sometimes happens to slaves with impulse control problems, or mental health issues, or other emotional difficulties where there is a combination of low self-awareness and high internal stress. It goes like this: The slave is having a rough time. Tension builds up inside them, and they are either too self-unaware to notice, or they haven't been given any way to release it. Eventually, they explode in a burst of bad behavior. The master is furious and punishes them, often with something corporal. The punishment is terrible, but after having a good screaming-and-crying session, they feel much lighter and more relieved. Their unconscious (if not their conscious) mind takes note of this – "I acted out and there was relief afterwards!" and you can bet the pattern will continue. The best way to deal with this sort of slave is to train them in self-awareness so that they can interrupt the pattern before the explosion, and ask the master to please provide them with a catharsis that is not linked to any specific behavior.

✦ **It pleases the master.** It is not lost on a slave when the master enjoys punishing them, if only for the surge of righteous wrath in a safe and virtuous context. It does seem to be lost on many masters, however, that enjoying the punishment (or the wrath) in any way is a big reinforcement to any slave who is heavily invested in making their master happy.

✦ **It's hot.** While we aren't talking about sceneplay "funishment" here – as in pretend punishments that are actually things the slave might enjoy – some slaves are able to eroticize any awful thing that they are forced to do, because being forced to do it is a reification of the power dynamic, and that's sexy. It should go without saying that arousal is most definitely a secondary gain, and it's not going to encourage behavioral changes.

- ✦ **It's romantic.** Slaves who are more about emotion than raw sex may secretly (or not-so-secretly) enjoy having a little mental scenario of themselves as the poor abused creature, suffering for their master, and any punishment that allows them to indulge in this fantasy is not going to be effective.

- ✦ **It gives an alternate option.** For some slaves, the fact that they'll get punished when they do some forbidden action merely sends them into a whirl of strategic calculation as to whether the punishment is something they're willing to endure if they really want that tempting thing bad enough. It "legitimizes" the option of doing it anyway and getting punished far more than a simple blanket "That's never OK, and if you do it, you're breaking the trust of the relationship, and letting the Team down, and being bad at your job." Transparency, and an order to come discuss things as soon as tempting thoughts begin, can head this off at the pass.

If you want to have punishment in a Teamwork model, both parties have to scrutinize the process for any of these secondary gains. That requires a lot of self-honesty and transparency on the part of the slave, as well as a perceptive eye on the part of the master. If the slave is experiencing any of these, you both need to change things. If none of our suggestions below seem to help, you may want to forgo punishment entirely, and keep some "funishment" for bedroom scenes.

If you don't utilize a punishment context at all, you may still inadvertently trigger some of the secondary gains above, especially if the there is a lot of emotion and attention around the necessary processing. However, this can be counteracted by having regular check-in communication sessions scheduled whether or not there is a problem, and giving out plenty of attention – and approval – at those. If the slave is already getting regular doses of attention, assessment, constructive criticism, and approval, there will be less motivation to force the issue with bad behavior.

Behavior modification should be seen by both parties as being useful, and both parties should be equally committed to the idea. It's not enough for the master to believe that it's worthwhile. The slave, too, has to be on board with it. All types of training should be seen by the slave as useful, even when they are difficult. A slave who doesn't like the idea of becoming someone who is more effective at their position and more pleasing to their master may lack commitment to the relationship, or may have deep damage to their self-esteem and their ability to believe in change for the better, especially for themselves.

If neither of these are the case, and the master has trouble getting the slave on board with the idea of ongoing behavior modification, the best course is to ask the slave to suspend judgment and go along with it because it pleases the master to try. At the very least, they should be able to commit to wholeheartedly helping the master with his new "hobby" of changing them, even if they don't believe that it can be done. This gives the master enough time to establish a track record of actual change, after which a reasonably perceptive slave will be able to see that change is possible and desirable.

It isn't just slaves who need behavior modification. Masters aren't perfect either, and they may have trouble being effective in all areas of their life, including their M/s relationships. While it's true that many masters have absolutely no interest in self-improvement, and really don't think it's relevant to them, we personally feel that the word "mastery" includes mastery of self as well as another. Part of mastering one's self is continually working to be a more effective human being. Besides, it's good for the slave to see the master bothering with self-improvement. It makes it feel like more of a team effort, and provides them with a good example.

However, it is not the slave's job to change the master in any way. The slave needs to learn to adapt to the master, not try to alter them to make the slave's job easier. Instead, the master has the option of using the slave as a tool to change themselves. That tool can be shaped and refined, personally designed to be more effective. Masters, in general, tend to be stubborn people who don't like to be told what to do. (If they did like to be told what to do, they might be on the other side of the slash.) If a master feels that their slave is making unwelcome attempts to change them – often in the form of nagging – they need to remember that they have the power to change that behavior and turn it to their own uses.

As an example, let's say that you, the master, know that you should exercise more. However, your attempts to make yourself do it have generally failed. You don't like or can't afford a gym, but you know that you exercise best when you've got a buddy to do it with. However, you aren't sure you'll be able to come through on it often enough to want to involve a friend who may be disappointed when you blow it off. On the other hand, you've got a slave to help you if you want it. You just have to personally design the form in which the help should appear.

First, honestly assess what it will take to get you to do this. How often should your slave ask you if you'd like to exercise? Under what circumstances? What times of day or situations would be an absolute failure? What phrasing will be least likely to irritate you, and most likely to get you past your reluctance in the moment? What tone of voice will sound least like nagging? Is there a physical position or body language the slave can use that will reinforce the dynamic and keep you from feeling resentful? What attitude should the slave maintain during the difficult period of exercise, especially if you seem unhappy with the whole thing? If you snap at them, are they permitted to remind you that they are acting on orders? Alternately, should they just assume you remember that too, but need to vent your irritation somewhere, and spewing it at a target that won't take it personally is another service they can provide? Would they be able to provide that service, or is that not something they are capable of at this point?

If you aren't sure about the answers to each of these questions, you're probably not alone. Many of us were not raised to think deeply about what behavior in others motivates us most effectively. Instead of sitting around feeling confused, use your slave to help you experiment. ("...Today, ask me this way. Tomorrow, ask me that way.") If you do this, however, be sure to let the slave know why you're asking it, so that they are less likely to take it personally if their attempts are met with growls.

When I first went through this process of designing my slave's actions to be the most effective tool I could use to push myself through difficult situations, I worried that all these "cushioning" protocols were simply coddling my ego. However, I eventually came to accept that if I didn't try to make the process as pleasant as possible, it simply wouldn't work. By adjusting my slave's attitude, phrasing, and general demeanor, I created the circumstances under which I could best improve myself. Of course, this required brutal self-honesty, which is part of the master's path anyway.

Don't be afraid to use your slave to remind you about things you tend to forget, or motivate you to do things you dislike, or ask you not to do things that are bad for you. The key to keeping resentment about the activity from coloring your feelings toward your slave is to design their aid to be as respectful as possible. This may also include orders to go away quietly and not take it personally if you decide to ignore their programmed suggestion today. Doing it this way will reify the dynamic rather than undercut it, as anything that verges on "nagging" may do. Refraining from nagging is especially difficult for female slaves who have been caretakers in their lives, and it may take specific instructions – and perhaps a role-play run-through – to make sure that they get the idea. However, you're the master and it's your responsibility. If you don't like the way that your tool is acting, it's time to rehone its edge the way you like. Keep reminding yourself that you have that power. Keep reminding your slave that it is in their best interest to remain respectful as well.

Alternatives To Punishment

Punishment does not necessarily have to be adversarial – and it is possible to use punishment carefully in a Teamwork relationship – but it is almost impossible to have an adversarial relationship without it. One of the drawbacks to adversarial relationships is that they can sometimes discourage complete honesty, not to mention the kind of transparency that is required for a smoothly-running M/s relationship. This is especially the case when, in the slave's conscious or unconscious mind, punishment results from getting caught rather than from the undesired behavior itself. There's also that many "traditional" punishments are fairly disconnected from the "crime", or have only an arbitrary connection.

For the first time a particular error comes up, I usually don't do anything but talk about it, and assume that it was a mistake. I tell my slave, "For future reference, I want X." If it recurs, that's the time to think about consequences. If the master feels that some kind of artificial consequence is necessary, some alternatives may be:

✦ **"Natural" consequences.** Or as close to them as the master can get, especially if the misbehavior has real-world effects. As an example, one stay-at-home slave who ran up unnecessary charges that his master could ill afford to pay was sent down the road to the burger palace to be a whopper flopper for a few weeks to earn money for the bill.

✦ **Limits can be set as preventatives, not punishments.** The master should make sure to emphasize that this is the case. For two months running you mouthed off at that annoying person at the munch, and shamed me in public. It's clear that you're having trouble controlling yourself in those circumstances. You're placed in silence for the duration of this month's munch; you can say hello, but not much more. This is not to punish you, but to protect you from making an idiot of yourself again. Or: You have panic attacks and freak out when you drink caffeine. So no caffeine for you.

+ **The slave must not benefit in any way from their misbehavior.** Remember to keep down any instance of secondary gains. A good example of this principle involved a slave who went to the store to buy the master some ice cream; they were out of the master's favorite flavor, but instead or calling home or going to another store (both actions that the master had expressed a preference for in the past), the slave brought home their own favorite flavor. The master decided that the neighbors next door would probably love that flavor of ice cream, and sent the slave over to gift it to them.

+ **Behavioral conditioning can be used to break longstanding habits.** One slave wore a rubber band on his wrist for a week, with orders to snap it against his skin when he habitually said "um", "like", or "whatever". Another got slapped every time she made unnecessary apologies or self-criticisms, and had to think of three positive things to say instead. These types of techniques work well with some slaves and not so well with others; know your property and don't try to condition around past trauma. The ideal is to have immediate negative consequences that will be associated directly with the offending action. Punishment that happens long after the action can be effective in some cases, but often does not have the same effect.

✦ **Find ways to make micromanaging supervision easier for the master and less rewarding for the slave.** For example, if a slave does a lousy job at the dishes, the master can stand over them and watch them do each dish ... or the master can sit around playing a video game and largely ignoring the slave, and the slave has to wash each dish, bring it over for a brief inspection, and then be sent back to put it away or do it over. This also trains self-assessment.

✦ **Go back to a dramatically remedial stage of the skill.** This is probably my favorite, because it works well with a slave like mine who has a strong sense of "I'll show you!" (As a wise person once said about nerds becoming CEOs, "Never underestimate the power of 'I'll show you!'") Just regress the skill to its most remedial, mitten-strings aspect. *Obviously you can't handle remembering things, and you can't even handle writing them all down in a notebook, because you lose the notebook. So you're going to wear the notebook around your neck until you get to the point where it's second nature to remember it. Or: You are apparently incapable of showing up on time, so you're going to aim for an hour early, and sit in the car.* There is a bit of humiliation to this solution, which is annoying, and very difficult to do wrong. It is made even more effective if you can get the slave to help figure out the most remedial level of the skill.

This last method could also be referred to as "reducing expectations", and it is especially good for slaves who play the game that my wife refers to as "creative applied incompetence" – the idea that if they do a poor enough job at something, they might be relieved of having to do it again. Making them do the same job but in a more remedial way is the opposite of what they're looking for. However, it fails when applied to slaves who actually do want to do as little as possible, and would rather endure a remedial job than have to put in effort. Some creative applied incompetence types would actually rather put up with all manner of humiliation than actually do their jobs; these individuals may need a more adversarial dynamic, or they may need a complete reevaluation as to whether this is the job (or master) for them at all. It will also be ineffective for a slave who has no personal investment in whether they are doing a good job, or for whom the major assumed benefit of a power dynamic is the hope that they will not have to take responsibility for anything. However, we've covered most of these types back in the section on who is appropriate for a Teamwork dynamic, so let's assume that the slave in question is actually invested in doing well, but is having some problems applying themselves to it.

Ideally, you should gradually work up in stages to a less remedial form of the activity. There's more to this method than mere humiliation, though. As you slowly increase the level of responsibility involved, they are bound to pass through the point where they made the mistake before, and the difficulty can be better calibrated, isolated, and solved. If the slave is the sort who is likely to be damaged rather than motivated by a vague implied insult to their competence, it may be useful to emphasize that this is calibration and not arbitrary at all.

Eventually, when the slave understands the nature of this calibration, they may even come to a point of being able to humbly collude with the master on reducing and then raising expectations. After all, it is pretty frustrating to be certain that you can handle an order, only to continually fail at it. Sometimes the slave refuses to believe that they are less than competent at some parts of the situation, and it's the master's job to back them up until the glitchy area can be seen. This is a failure of pride and humility on the slave's part as much as a failure of competence, but if they see that the method works – even if it is painful – they may come to a place of being willing to work on it as part of the Team, rather than just seeing it as vague punishment.

> *Dear Sir: I've been thinking about the kind of string that I should use to hang that notebook I keep losing. May I suggest a shock collar? … In other news, I left my phone on the train today. Luckily, when I went back, someone had returned it to the security guard and I was able to collect it. Sigh. Maybe it can hang next to the notebook on the shock collar.*
>
> *– An email from V-boy, my ADD sub*

Checklist For Errors

In M/s pornography, there's often an assumption that slaves should be punished for any failure to achieve a desired result, regardless of why it went wrong. This assumption is often accompanied by the figure of a dominant of either gender who is implacably irrational about failure, doesn't want to know why it happened, and thinks that reacting angrily is all that is required to fix the problem. Real-life masters, on the other hand, know that real life has an unending supply of curve balls to pitch at the most enthusiastic and obedient servant. When the slave makes an error and it is not clearly deliberate disobedience, you may want to go through this checklist of questions to find out where things went sideways.

- ✦ **Were you aware of the request?** I know that my own slave often misses commands in a busy environment when we're both moving from room to room. I may see him hurrying off and assume that he's going to complete the order, when he's actually chasing the dog or checking the pot on the stove.

- ✦ **Were you aware that it was an order, not a suggestion?** This depends on how it is phrased. I tend to be sloppy when it comes to phrasing orders, and they can sometimes be mistaken for suggestions. That's why we have a specific protocol: the words "Yes, Sir" are spoken in response to anything the slave believes may be an order. This allows me to know that they understood it as such. It also allows me to stop him if it wasn't meant as an order ("…No, I was just thinking about ice cream, I don't actually want some right now…"), and allows him to ask about unclear phrasing with a simple intonation ("…uh, yes, Sir?"). Creating a similarly useful protocol for yourselves may clear up errors on this step.

✦ **Did you understand the order?** This includes the time frame, the desired outcome, etc. It's all very well and good for a master to be mysterious about the big picture, but this can result in misunderstandings and wrong directions on the slave's part.

✦ **Did you remember it? Why not?** Sometimes all that is required is for the slave to give the order their full attention. If that isn't enough, the Team needs to work out some type of effective reminder or cue. In some cases the master may be happy to provide ongoing reminders, but often it is beneficial if the slave eventually develops methods they can use without the master's direct assistance. It is also good to look at whether there is a pattern to what sort of orders get forgotten, or under what circumstances.

✦ **Did you have the resources to do the job? Did you allocate them properly?** This can include time, money, energy, and health, as well as physical-object resources. Some slaves are just lousy at managing time or money, and others tend to overestimate how much they can do in a day. Failure at this stage can indicate a need for special training in time management, or having the slave assess and report their energy levels several times per day until they learn to be more accurate with them. "Ran out" of time/money/etc. is often a priorities issue. This leads to the next question:

+ **Did you fail to accurately prioritize the order?**
  If the failure is here, it's time for a discussion
  of the master's priorities, to which slaves need
  to adapt themselves. The slave might think
  that the master's priorities are stupid (in
  which case they need to understand that they
  need to obey anyway), or they may not fully
  understand them, in which case the master
  needs to spell them out. There also may be the
  problem of the slave procrastinating on a task
  they don't want to do.

+ **Did a complication come up that you weren't
  sure how to handle?** We live on a small farm
  in New England, and the soil here is largely
  piled on top of glacial morain. This means
  that no matter how well you plowed up the
  rocks last year, there will be more next spring
  rising up from underneath. The common
  saying about attempting to dig on New
  England farms is "There's always a rock." This
  has become the defining statement for dealing
  with complications in our lives: *Of course
  there's a rock. There's always a rock. Assume
  that there will be complications. Make extra
  plans just in case. If you thought through
  possible rocks and made contingency plans,
  but the one rock you didn't consider was the
  one that appeared, learn from the experience
  and move on. Again: What can we do to
  prevent this from happening in the future?*

Study Questions

1. What methods has the master tried to modify the slave's behavior? How successful were these methods?

2. What methods has the master used to modify his own behavior? How successful have these methods been?

3. What non-adversarial approach might the Team use to modify the slave's most troublesome behavior?

4. What non-adversarial approach might the Team use to help the master modify their most troublesome behavior?

Part 4:
Arguing!

Being Right Versus Being Effective

In BDSM porn, and in BDSM porn-based models, there are a lot of silly rules dedicated to making the master look right, and making the slave continually pretend that the master is right, even when they are heading for a cliff. (Of course, the BDSM porn generally also has either superhuman masters who never err, or psychopaths who aren't going to keep their slaves alive for long anyway.) In real life, of course, people on both sides make errors. We don't personally know any long-term full-time slaves who believe that their masters are never wrong about anything ... and honestly, we don't know any who wouldn't respect a master less for wanting them to pretend that wrong turn wasn't really a wrong turn.

Masters should, ideally, be confident in themselves and their right to be in authority over someone who submits to them, even though they are flawed human beings. A master's authority is not based on them being flawless; it's based on that slave deciding that this master's judgment is good enough, overall, to be worth following. This implies that the slave is willing to endure the occasional error in exchange for a worthy place to put their submission.

If the master is emotionally secure in their position, acknowledging a mistake doesn't damage their mastery ... and if it damages them in the eyes of the slave, they've got a slave with completely unrealistic ideas of what a real live master is like, rather than a fantasy cardboard cut-out. Pretending that the master is always right means that both parties believe that the master is weak, and too emotionally fragile to handle a simple offer of correct information. Mastery requires a sturdy ego, and one sign of a sturdy ego is the ability to say, "Yup, that was a mistake. I'll take responsibility for cleaning up the mess, and I'll do things differently next time. Now let's move on."

However, the key term in the last paragraph is "a simple offer of correct information." While it may be a sign of insecurity for a master to refuse to hear any idea that they might not always be correct, it is a sign of disrespect for a slave to offer their opinion in any way that takes satisfaction in "getting one over on the master", or is exasperated, or sarcastic, or snide, or angry. It is perfectly reasonable for a master to set limits on the way in which a potential course correction can be offered. This isn't done to coddle the master's ego – it's done to remind the slave of their position, and why they chose it in the first place.

This is based on one of those lessons that thoughtful people learn early on, but some people never do absorb properly: it's better to be effective than to be "right". We put "right" in quotes because the real problem isn't being correct in one's information, but in needing to have one's correctness acknowledged in an emotionally satisfying way. Being able to say, "I'm right and you're wrong!" and have that be humbly acknowledged by the other party is something we're taught to want, regardless of our position on a power exchange scale. In most cases, however, presenting the information in that way is the least effective method of actually making any change in someone else's behavior.

Perceptive people figure out quickly that it's better to choose the words or actions that have the greatest potential for actually being acted on, even if those words or actions aren't the ones that are the most emotionally satisfying. Some people, however, continue to prioritize their emotional needs for validation – which may include venting, needing sympathy, or needing a show of penitence from the other person – over making any real change in the situation. If those people are in a power dynamic relationship, it can go very badly.

This is especially (although not exclusively) true if it's the slave who prioritizes being able to feel "right" over being actually effective. A slave is in a precarious position with regard to being "right" when their master is "wrong". On an emotional level, if they're proven right and their master was in the wrong, they get the satisfaction of knowing that they were right ... but also the knowledge that they've committed themselves to following someone whose judgment was wrong, and this can lead to the creeping feeling that they are unsafe, and creeping disrespect for the person they've pledged themselves to. If they're proven wrong and their master turns out to be right, they're annoyed, but safe.

So what ought a slave to do, knowing that they will eventually face their master's mistakes? First, they should *want* their master to be right. If the master and the slave are in a standoff, the slave should not be hoping for that moment of "Ha ha, I'm right and you're wrong," on any level. Being in that space is corrosive to a power dynamic. Instead, they should aim for one of two attitudes:

A) I'm scared and distressed because this behavior is making me feel unsafe. Please, Ma/am/Sir, help me to feel less unsafe about it. Convince me that my worries are unfounded, or that it's all going to work out, or that you're seeing a bigger picture than I am. *(Note: If the problem doesn't really warrant feeling scared and unsafe, don't try to talk yourself into it in order to justify arguing! We'll talk more about that temptation in the next chapter, where we discuss inadvertently encouraging emotional "arson".)*

B) I respect my master, and I believe in their ability to extract us from any blind alley they happen to lead us into. I want to be helpful, and the best way I can be helpful is to offer alternatives in the most neutral (or cheerful, or however your master likes it) way, and work on being a serene Team partner if my suggestions are not taken.

(This is, of course, assuming that the slave does trust the master's competence in that way. If they don't, then there is a deeper problem that needs to be discussed, far beyond the effective and appropriate way to point out a difference of opinion.)

Some s-types will already be bridling at the idea of censoring their emotional responses in any way, even in the name of "respectful behavior". After all, don't we encourage the master to know everything about their slave's emotions? Don't we continually emphasize transparency and pontificate about how a master can't create the proper environment for their slave unless they know everything that's going on with them? Yes, we certainly do. However, informing the master of an emotional state does not mean acting it out on the spot. There are many ways to get that information across; acting it out is only one of them, and often not the most effective one. Saying, "Sir/Ma'am, I'm feeling scared and upset about this" is a long way away from exploding into an unraveling maelstrom of hysteria.

On an even smaller level, we don't believe that the emotions behind sarcasm, snideness, and eye-rolling frustration need to be acted out, ever. When a slave enacts these verbal behaviors, it slowly corrodes their respect for their master, and their desire to be a slave. Refraining from expressing these petty emotions never harmed anyone, and knowing that those behaviors are not acceptable can remind the slave that they are, indeed, held to a higher standard of behavior whether they like it or not – which can be a powerful and satisfying reminder of their position.

Most of the masters that we know would rather be informed of their slave's negative emotions in a manner that didn't insist on acting them out in full color, right there in the middle of the department store. If the slave honestly believes that the master has a track record of ignoring more respectful attempts to communicate a problem, and nothing gets done until the slave explodes, this is a subject to discuss. Masters need to understand that by ignoring less intrusive attempts to call attention to negative emotions, they are conditioning for those explosions. Remember that Teamwork is behavior modification; don't reward behavior that you don't want to see again, and remember to reward the slave when they get it right.

It's in a master's best interest to honestly and realistically assess the most effective way that a slave can make a suggestion, offer a dissenting opinion, or express a negative emotion. If you're a master and you're considering this issue, you owe it to yourself to be completely self-honest. What kind of response will be least triggering? What wording, tone of voice, or body language will make you feel like your slave is a helpful junior Team member, not a scornful opponent? How can your slave say hard and painful things to you, and not have to censor any of the information, but do it in a way that you will find easiest to hear?

You have the right to demand this (although with it comes the obligation to properly train your slave to do it without using voice restrictions as an excuse to hold back information). If it makes you a more effective part of the Team – if, for example, it makes you better able to hear your slave's thoughts, feelings, and mindset – then it could be said that you have an obligation to the Team to work on it. Even slaves who object to censorship of attitude – perhaps through laziness, perhaps through a fear that they will not be able to find a way to sincerely communicate an emotion without physically expressing it – eventually find that if a change of behavior gets them heard more often and more effectively, it's worth doing.

Slaves who identify strongly with their emotions and with their emotional volatility might also see being told to control their affect as a rejection of who they are. "But I'm just an intense person, and when I scream at you, I'm just expressing my intensity. If you really love me for who I am, you'll accept me when I act like that." The answer for this situation might be a long slow climb toward the idea that their volatile emotions are just something they have (and can control), not something which defines who they are, or that controls them.

Study Questions

1. Think of a recent situation where the slave struggled with wanting to be "right" rather than being obedient.
2. Why was being "right" in this situation so important to the slave? Was it the principle of the situation, or fear of a bad outcome, or a struggle with priorities, or past training, or something else?
3. Who has the stronger emotional investment in this situation?
4. How do you both feel about how the situation worked out? How would you feel if it had worked out differently?
5. What is, or what would be, the slave's reaction to finding out that they were wrong in this situation? Relieved? Annoyed?
6. What factors might pressure the master to "give in", even when they don't want to? Clear evidence that they are wrong? The slave's distress? Wanting to see the slave happy? Something else?
7. What are the Team's priorities and goals in this situation? Obedience? Reification of the dynamic? Optimizing the outcome?
8. What tools can both people use to achieve this next time? How can you prompt each other to use these tools?

Approaching Conflict

The idea that masters and slaves never fight is ... well, not true for any of the long-term M/s couples we know personally. It's true that the ability of the master to shut the slave up at will can become an ability to avoid arguments – and it's also true that "Because I said so – and you agreed to do whatever I said," can be a valid point to cut off disagreement in the heat of the moment. However, slaves do have to be able to bring up their negative feelings about life situations, and masters do need to listen. We've already strongly suggested beginning such a discussion with the point that We The Team will try to fix what can be fixed, but even that won't stop conflict. Even the most well-oiled machine of an M/s couple will sometimes wish the other person would drop through a sudden hole opening up in the earth.

One problem that we had was that I am a busy person, and I don't always have time for Joshua's problems on demand. When I am busy with one of my demanding jobs and Joshua brings some personal problem to my attention, my attitude is often, "Is it on fire? No? Then it can wait until later tonight, or tomorrow, or some later scheduled time." If Joshua was in serious distress I was more likely to drop what I was doing – if it was remotely possible to drop it – and deal with Joshua's emotions on the spot. Over time, however, we discovered that this encouraged Joshua to unconsciously scale up his feelings over the situation. If being on fire got him attention, he'd figure out a way to be on fire. Guaranteeing him immediate attention depending on how distressed he seemed simply encouraged him to continually commit emotional arson.

A useful way of handling this sort of problem is for the master to point out that although this is acknowledged to be an issue, it's not a high enough priority to address right this moment. The master can point out that it's the slave's job to absorb and accept the master's priorities, not the other way around. This only works if A) the master actually does put time aside to deal with the problem, on their own time but eventually; B) the slave has seen the master assure them that something will be dealt with and then actually get to it; and C) the master has looked deeply into the problem and is absolutely sure that the slave is committing arson, not that they are legitimately traumatized.

With a particularly emotionally volatile slave, this discernment may need to be done past the slave's protestations – if they've gotten into the habit of convincing themselves that a situation is more traumatizing than it is because of secondary gains, it may be a hard habit to unlearn. And, of course, the master needs to understand the difference between a slave with a bad habit that is getting the better of them, and a slave with a serious impairment that requires assessment and special treatment. However, we'll cover that in the section on impairments.

Slaves aren't the only ones who sometimes prioritize unconscious emotional satisfaction over effectiveness. In some relationships, it seems that what the master wants is a place where they can feel righteous anger and actually act on it. We've seen some adversarial dynamics where the slave knows on some level that giving the master a venue to be openly angry at someone and act on that wrath is a much-needed service, perhaps as a release for all the places in the master's life where they can't show anger or act it out. In these cases, a punishment dynamic is implicitly (although rarely explicitly) a service to the master, and the slave gets the benefit of knowing that even extreme imperfection in the slave's behavior will please the master on some level. For these masters, saying, "Why don't you just beat them when you feel like beating them, without all the punishment games?" doesn't work, because a significant portion of their pleasure comes from being allowed to safely indulge in righteous anger.

That being said, there are many other sorts of agendas behind an argument, and sometimes ignorance about those agendas simply prolongs the fight, as one person attempts repeatedly to give the other person something that wasn't what they wanted. Knowing what your partner wants as an outcome can help bring closure at a quicker pace. Even if you don't want to give them what they hope to get, you won't waste time and energy giving them a gift they'll refuse.

We created this little chart of possible motivations so that arguing couples could pick it up and ask, "What do you want out of this? What do you hope happens? What will you settle for?" Start by looking at the list, together, before you actually get into a conflict. Then, separately, write down your five top motivations during an argument, and then – even more importantly – write down what you believe that your partner's top five motivations are.

Then compare your lists. Understand that the ideal is not to have the same motivations – most people don't, and that's fine – but to see how well you know your partner's priorities during an argument. If you were right on, great – you know them well. If you didn't guess them right, then you've got a lot of talking to do. Keep this list in mind when you're actually arguing, so that your conflict can be more useful to the relationship.

When we come into conflict, my motivations tend to be:
1) To be able to express my feelings on the matter, even if I can't have my way.
2) Getting my way.
3) To be able to convince you that I am right.
4) For you to convince me that I am wrong.
5) To convince others that I'm right and/or you're wrong.
6) Getting an apology.
7) Wanting you to feel bad about what you did.
8) Showing you that you've made an error.
9) Confirming that I have a right to feel upset.
10) Convincing me that you won't do it again.
11) To help you understand my reasons or motivations, and thus know me better.
12) To get emotional support in doing what I have to do.
13) For you to push/force/seduce me into doing what is necessary.
14) To brainstorm possible solutions.
15) Other:

Of course, most arguments in a M/s relationship aren't about huge important issues where the master's errors will cause death and/or disaster. Most are about the little things – how much money is being paid for that brand of bologna, or which car insurance to buy, or whether that pair of jeans is too far gone to be seen in public. Even if there are large issues that are not being discussed, the underground conflict often surfaces as arguments about those small differences of opinion, because they're safer.

A good slave wants the best and highest service for their master. The problem comes when the slave has one idea about what the best and highest manifestation of any order should look like, and the master has a different one. While the master may take the slave's information into account, they are not obligated to do so – and sometimes the slave forgets, in their pursuit of perfecting the process, just how much masters like to be obeyed. Sometimes it means more to the master to have it done in the way that they envisioned than to have it done the "best" way. As Joshua eventually discovered, "I might gain five points by suggesting a better way, but I lost twenty points by not just saying, 'Yes, sir,' making it completely clear that I was ready and willing to do it exactly his way, and then suggesting my alteration as a possibility that I wasn't heavily invested in seeing happen. Sometimes what makes him happiest is just my obedience."

Criteria for Superiority

The topic of "superiority" is a tricky one. Whenever it gets brought up in M/s circles, it seems that there is a chorus of people deliberately and fearfully misunderstanding the concept and thinking that someone is trying to prove that all masters are inherently and cosmically superior to all slaves. That isn't what we're saying here at all. In fact, we'd like to leave cosmic grading entirely out of the equation.

What we mean is that nearly every slave has some internal scale by which they have judged their master to be superior – to other masters, at least, if not to the entirety of humanity. They've chosen to serve them because of those traits. The few exceptions to this rule – the handful of slaves we've spoken with who don't consider their masters to be superior human beings in any way – are generally a small percentage of those couples who were married for a long time in an egalitarian relationship before one partner decided that they wanted to be a slave, and the other one gradually agreed to be their master. While many of those couples still see their spouse-master to be superior in some way, there are a few who don't, and simply love and serve their partners anyway.

However, the majority of slaves will, if pushed, come up with a list of reasons why their master is one of the most wonderful people in the world, or at least in their life. That list will usually have nothing to do with any cosmic reality about who is the bigger mote of dust in the eyes of the Universe. It will be entirely personal and subjective, and every slave's list will be different. For some, physical strength and size will be important; others couldn't care less and are happy with a partner in a wheelchair. For some, their master must be smarter than them, or a better psychologist and judge of character. For others, their strong moral fiber is on the list. Honor, self-control, social status, life experience, financial stability, and good judgment may also find their way onto the list. It's likely that each list has quite a few characteristics, and that the master they've signed up with has most of them, or they wouldn't be following him or her.

In the beginning of the relationship, it's a good idea for the master to lean hard on the qualities that the slave finds superior in them. Especially early on, it's a good way to help make the master's authority real to the slave, and not a game. One is reminded of Henry Ford, who pointed out that asking who should be the leader in the group is like asking who should be the tenor in the quartet – of course, the man who sings tenor.

But what happens when there are a few characteristics on that "superiority list" that the master can't fill? What if the slave is better at some things than the master, and uses those traits to negatively judge the person they are supposed to be trusting? It's not unusual for those traits to be ones that the slave strongly values in themselves, a building block for their self-esteem. For the master to devalue it in themselves is, sometimes, seen as a way to devalue the slave and their qualities. If the slave is projecting their criteria negatively on the master, there are a few ways to handle the problem.

One option is that the master *can* actually discount the importance of those qualities without devaluing them in the slave. It's all right to say, "I don't need to be bigger and stronger than you. You'll do as I say because I said so, not because I won some macho chest-thumping contest." Then you need to make it clear that those qualities are good and useful in a slave, but irrelevant in this particular master. Stress that the relationship between the two of you is complementary rather than the joining of two identical people (which is true, anyway). Don't engage them on their own ground. For example, if you have a lawyerly slave who can find loopholes in anything, refuse to argue with them when they get into that mood. Just say, "I don't care what you think about my reasoning right now. Your job is to do what I say, period." This method can be effective, but it can stray into being somewhat adversarial.

Conversely, in the Teamwork model you can point out that while those qualities might be nice for you to personally have, you do actually have access to them – because you own your slave, and they have those qualities. In this model, the master says, "I have you to do that. I can use you to do that. In fact, I do actually have that talent, because I have you, and you are my resource. I don't have to be good at doing your job." This brings it back around to the We Are A Team song.

It took us many years to figure out that neither of us are really any good at each others' jobs. Sometimes we would become angry at each other for perceived "incompetence", but we eventually figured out that most of the time, this happened when one of us was doing the other person's job. Our lives are complicated, and we both have finite time and energy. Sometimes a job comes up that we didn't plan for, and it needs to get done right away by whoever has their hands free. If it was a job that I would have normally assigned to my slaveboy because it was more congruent with his skillsets, but I ended up having to do it ... well, my efforts were usually adequate, but generally never up to the standards that he would have achieved. Rather than seeing this as sheer incompetence on my part, he did eventually learn to tell himself, "Well, of course he's not as good as I am at my job! He's good enough for an emergency situation, and under better circumstances I'd just take care of that. Hopefully next time will be better circumstances!"

Similarly, while my slaveboy is good at problem-solving, and he can be in charge of projects and lead people if necessary, he doesn't enjoy it and has no illusions that he is better at long-term planning or making hard decisions than me. He and my second boy have often joked that making the decisions is the real scut-work, and they're very glad that they can generally relax and let their master handle that. I've also learned that if my slaveboy is put in charge of an elaborate project while I am off doing something else, I have to accept that his on-the-fly decisions might not be exactly up to my standards, but they are generally good enough to bridge the gap in an emergency.

On the other hand, a master should not be afraid to use every inch of their slave as a resource. Slaves often have all kinds of hidden talents. Some may lie buried within them, undiscovered even by themselves until the master's sharp eyes notice that they have a knack for it – and it behooves the master to be that sharp-eyed about noticing their slave's knacks. Some skills or talents may be known to the slave, but it doesn't occur to them to bring it up, perhaps because those skills don't fall in with "traditional slave work" and they don't believe that they could possibly be useful to a master. (It took ten months before I learned that my second boy was an excellent artist, largely for that reason.) Remember that there's no skill or talent of theirs that it is inappropriate to use if you want it. If you're stumped for an answer and your slave is good at problem solving, there's no shame in using them. Their perspective is yours to plunder.

Study Questions

1. What types of situations tend to make you come into conflict with each other?
2. How does the master tend to approach these conflicts?
3. How does the slave tend to approach these conflicts?
4. What would you consider an ideal way to approach these conflicts?
5. Given who you are, and who your partner is, what is the cleanest way that the Team can approach a conflict?
6. Which ways are most destructive to your relationship? What motivation is the highest priority for each of you to stop doing?
7. What fights do you have over and over again?
8. If you assume that this means you're probably not speaking the same language, what can the Team do to get some translations?
9. What subjects are difficult for you to bring up with your partner? What makes it difficult? Are those good reasons?
10. Is there a protocol that can be invoked to make it easier to talk about these things?

Part 5: Impairments

When Someone Has An Impairment

This subject is more specifically handled in our continually growing series of books on disabilities in power dynamic relationships (available at www.alfredpress.com), but part of taking responsibility for one's part in the relationship is taking responsibility for one's physical and mental glitches. This means being solidly in reality about everyone's disabilities, even the small ones. Whether some of them can eventually be overcome is irrelevant to the present moment; they must be compensated for rather than denied while they still exist. This includes masters as well as slaves being realistic about their problems, and building compensatory mechanisms into the Team protocol for those as well.

In more than half the situations where someone comes to us for advice and the Teamwork method isn't working for them, it turns out that one or both of the people involved have some sort of physical, mental, or neurological glitch that has not been taken into account. When we gently (and sometimes hesitantly) point it out, the parties tend to shrug it off as if it "shouldn't make a difference". Well, in a perfect world perhaps it wouldn't, but we live in this world, and it's better to accept that it does. Sometimes the denial that causes that refusal to take an impairment into account comes from a long history of hopelessness around its effects, and a fear that if it is scrutinized too much, it will destroy this relationship as it has destroyed other parts of the individual's life.

However, while we do generally acknowledge that M/s relationships are somewhat more difficult to get right than egalitarian ones, they have a definite advantage when it comes to compensating for impairments. The hierarchy and structured format can become a kind of exoskeleton to hold both parties up when they would otherwise fall down. If you're going to have rules anyway, you might as well make rules that help everyone to deal with their problems as effectively as possible.

Impairments can come in a dizzying swath of variables, the ones that affect the M/s relationship – and the ability to do Teamwork – the most are the ones that impair judgment in any way. Does this master have trouble making good decisions when his blood sugar is low, which happens at least once a day if he's not constantly careful? Does this slave have ADD and retains instructions best if they are delivered with a hand on the arm? Does this master have chronic pain, perhaps with days when it overwhelms her judgment and she shouldn't do any mental "heavy lifting"? Does this slave have PTSD triggers around being slapped in the face due to a previous assault? Each of these issues can theoretically be improved by implementing a protocol. It's just a matter of finding the right ones.

On the other hand, it is also a difficult truth that the Teamwork model only functions when both master and slave come to the Team as functional, responsible adults. In the case of some mental illnesses, one member may not be able to come to the Team in the moment as a fully responsible adult. This is one of the rare situations where an M/s couple who would not normally want to be adversarial might have to go in that direction. (We'll go into these situations more deeply in our books *Broken Toys* and *Mastering Mind*, written by and for submissives and dominants respectively who have mental illnesses and neurological dysfunctions.)

In the book *Power Circuits: Polyamory In A Power Dynamic*, Master James writes: "A major element of my work as Master has been ensuring that (my slaves) make the medical choices they need to be healthy. Our culture teaches us that a head cold is cause for sympathy, but that an episode of rage, anger, or anxiety is a moral weakness even when it comes from a chemical spike. We are taught that people who need to be medicated are broken or sick. While I am a believer in people taking responsibility for their own shit, that can't happen unless everyone has a level playing field, and sometimes 'better living through chemistry' can help." While we are not suggesting that all mental illnesses can necessarily always be fixed through therapy and/or medications, his point about the level playing field is well put. One can't be a functional Team member if one is not functional, so brainstorming and experimenting with ways of compensating for impairments should be a top priority for the Team.

Owning an impaired slave can be a tricky thing if the master isn't prepared for it. Some glitches, of course, are more difficult than others, and we strongly emphasize that a master should not be penalized for rejecting a potential slave on the basis of not having the skill to handle their impairment. Rather than feeling betrayed, the would-be slave should instead feel as if they've dodged a bullet, and kept either party from wasting any further time on each other – time in which bad decisions could be made.

A master should never blame a slave for *being* impaired, but they can insist that the slave take responsibility for skillfully handling their impairment. When the slave is colliding the two concepts, the master can call them back to the lesson of "There's always a rock, and you need to think ahead about how the inevitable rock is going to affect you." The first piece of training to attack with a disabled slave is to teach them how to give regular and accurate assessments of their condition at any given time. This can be done through verbal reports at set times or on demand, paper charts, online messaging, or any other method, but the language and measurements used should be understood clearly by both parties. Without this information, the master can't make good decisions about how to manage the slave, especially if the situation is subject to change without notice due to medical problems. Assessment training can be particularly difficult with a slave who wants to pretend that they are less impaired than reality would show, or who is used to dissociating from the situation, but it's crucial to making things work. On their side, the master should keep in mind that being limited by the slave's disabilities is not compromising with your slave, but compromising with reality. (Some people use the terms "limits" versus "limitations", in order to indicate the flexibility of obstacles.) While a master is obligated to take a slave's limitations into account – or at least they'll be shooting themselves in the foot if they don't – the master is not necessarily obligated to do exactly what the slave tells them, as we'll discuss in a moment.

When a master has a slave with a disability of any sort, their first task is to learn anything they can about that disability. This can include reading about it in books or on the Internet, asking the slave to write them a detailed description, speaking with the slave's health care professionals, speaking with other people with this or similar disabilities, or (ideally) a combination of all of these. Care should be taken to discuss whether the master will be taking responsibility for the slave's body (and thus their medical care and healthy behaviors), or whether the slave will be retaining that responsibility themselves. The slave should not be pressured into giving that up if they aren't yet ready to trust the master with doing as well or better than they could handle it themselves, and the master should not be pressured into taking it if they don't feel like they can reasonably make those decisions. Learning everything possible about the impairment is still important even if the slave retains all decision-making ability on the matter, because the master needs every scrap of that information to make good decisions about effective handling of the slave.

If the master does end up with full responsibility for the slave's body and mind, having a thorough understanding of the situation is crucial. It's especially helpful if the master can find another M/s couple who have the same problem with their slave, but masters in this situation have reported that another surprisingly helpful source is parents of children with this disability. That's not because the slave is a child, but because it helps to hear people talk about how to make good decisions for someone in their care who is struggling with this issue – especially since it is an issue that they can't experience and understand from the inside, but need to make decisions around how to work with the slave anyway.

Regardless of who has responsibility for decisions around the slave's health, the hardest moment of all – and don't bet that you'll be lucky enough to avoid it, if you're in this situation – is the moment when the master and slave disagree over whether the slave is or is not impaired in a given situation, and to what extent. (In fact, if you haven't hit this situation yet, we suggest discussing what you'll do when you get there.) While the person with the impairment does know its effects best from an internal position, sometimes the perspective of long-term partners who see you every day can be useful, especially if the problem is one that does impair judgment when it's going on in full force. Partners can watch for warning signs and can sometimes know when you're going there before you actually cross into that area. They can also make inaccurate assumptions out of fear, of course, which should be taken into account. However, in the case of a master commenting on a slave's behavior, it is assumed that the slave already considers the master's judgment to be trustworthy enough to center their life around, so taking the master's opinion about their impairment seriously should not be too far a stretch.

Conversely, sometimes the slave reacts badly because they feel unheard by the master's assumptions. "I've lived in this body for my whole life, and now you're telling me that you know better about my limits than I do? Why can't you take my information about myself seriously? After all, I bust my ass to give you these continual reports, and now you're not taking them into account?" This is especially a problem if the slave has felt continually unheard about their condition in other areas of their life, and the master's trust has made them feel secure about discussing it. It's useful to have a very solid foundation of trust already established in other areas. We've already mentioned how the first few "real-world" areas of life where the M takes control should not be hot-button issues, and a disability is definitely one of those issues.

On the other side of things, one of the hardest parts of mastery is the constant risk assessment.

Masters depend on their slaves for thorough and honest information about their physical, mental, and emotional condition in order to make the best decisions possible, but what about the day when the master looks the slave in the eye and says, "I think you're wrong!" We're assuming here that the slave is not lying about their situation – which would be an entirely different argument – but honestly believes, with all their heart, that they can do X just fine or will be irrevocably harmed by Y ... and the master just doesn't believe that their self-assessment is correct.

The slave, in this moment, has only two choices – to trust, or to rebel. They can choose to trust the master to make the right decision – or, at least, to clean up the mess if they make the wrong decisions – or they can decide that they cannot trust the master's judgment on the matter, and take action. (If they are psychologically owned to the point where there is no recourse and no way to disobey, then there isn't any choice, but one assumes that they would not have come to that point without an immense amount of trust to be leaned on.) Before leaping to that decision, however, the slave may have a few other options. They might ask the master to look further and get a second opinion from an outside source. They might ask for an explanation of how repairs will happen if everything goes wrong. They could consider the master's track record of making good decisions in hard situations. They could ask for aid in coming to a place of trust. It's best if these options have already been discussed well before such a moment shows up, so if you haven't talked about them, it's time.

Risk assessment isn't easy. No master wants to screw up, especially with their slave's health or trust. There's agony in that moment – "Do I push them through it, and maybe break them, and damage their trust in me? Do I push them through it, knowing that if we triumph that it may change their self-image for the better? Do I back off and reinforce their self-image as a weak person? Do I back off and avoid a potential failure, but give up ever getting what I want in the situation, and end up feeling powerless as a master?" These options can put even the most experienced master into a 3 a.m. tailspin of indecision. However, as a master who is particularly terrified of failure, I can tell you that it's not a question of what to do *if* that moment comes, it's about *when*. That's why it should be discussed beforehand. Also, since risk assessment is part of the master's job, they need to get good at it … and they won't get good at it if they don't practice, and they can't practice without occasional failure. This means that it's best to practice on smaller issues before this big knot of trust and risk comes up around a major impairment. (The master may need years of observation to get to the point of being able to judge on that matter, anyway.)

One way to handle things is to get the slave colluding on getting the master to a point of skill with regard to the situation. The master can say, "I intend to make myself such an expert on you and your problems that I know them better than you do, and will be at least as effective in making decisions on them as you are, and hopefully more so. And you're going to help me to become that expert, in any way that we can figure out." It then becomes a Team project, with everyone on board with the eventual goal of the slave falling comfortably into that place of trust … because they helped it happen.

Brainstorming is, again, the Team's friend with regard to finding ways to cope. It's also a good assessment of how much the slave is really on board with the Team – do they participate eagerly in brainstorming and experimenting with potential ways to find compensations, or do they hold back and express disbelief that anything could ever work? Is their response enthusiastic and grateful, or a stream of excuses? Impairments can be a touchy and painful subject for anyone, but it's important for the slave to make the effort. In the worst cases, the Team may have to back up a step and ask, "What can we do to get you to an emotional place where you can feel good about brainstorming and experimenting, where you can find some hope that something can be done, if only a little? Let's make that a priority."

One simple but lovely example of brainstorming that we like to share is the tale of a slave who had a walking disability, and couldn't carry anything very far. Her master could have just let her off of all cleaning duties – "Never mind, we'll hire a maid, you're just not capable..." but instead they brainstormed a solution: she would have a multi-shelf cart on wheels to push around and collect items to put or throw away. This worked fine for every room except for the office, which was down a step. Instead of giving up on it, she came up with the idea of having a second cart for that room, so that she could transfer items from one to the other at the doorway. No matter what the problem might be, it's possible to find ways to compensate if everyone is willing to give it some thought. (And if you're really stuck, ask other people with similar issues and get a list of ideas from them.)

When the master is the one with the impairment, it's an even harder situation, for obvious reasons. While the master can – in some cases – force the slave to deal with their impairment in ways that are harmonious with the power dynamic, the slave has no way of forcing the master to do anything against their will without stepping outside the boundaries of the dynamic. Instead, it's the master's job to force themselves to deal with reality and build in compensations. That's part of the price we pay for being in charge.

However, the slave can be used as a resource in this matter. They can be called in as a respectful reminder service, medication delivery method, never-nagging cheerleader, or whatever else is needed to get the job done. Rather than a copout, the master should see this as efficient use of valuable resources – why try to cut that meat with your old pocket knife when you own an expensive cooking blade? The master also needs to be willing to brainstorm with the slave on possible solutions, and to implement experiments with the slave's help. the slave's job in this is to remain respectful, enthusiastic, and resilient in the face of their beloved master enduring painful failure. So long as the master is doggedly trying, they should never think less of them for failing, but should see their continued struggle as a sign of strength and worthiness.

As we've discussed in previous chapters, it's perfectly acceptable for the master to tailor the slave's behavior so as to push as few buttons as possible while getting the job done, and this is especially important when using the slave as a resource for impairment support. As an example, we've spoken to an M/s family where the master has bipolar disorder. Her standing orders are that in the event she has forgotten her medication and begins to act in an unstable way, her slaves are not to confront her about it, or even ask her if she has remembered her meds. Instead, a slave is to go into the bathroom and check the med minder, which is sorted by day of the week, and see if the meds have been taken. If they have been forgotten, the slave is to silently and discreetly leave them, along with a glass of water, within her line of sight. This way, the solution is not a challenge in any way, but simply pure service. Little courtesies such as this can be soothing to a master who wants desperately to be in control, but who is painfully aware and constantly fighting against the outside factors trying to overpower them. A master with a serious impairment probably already grapples with blows to their confidence and sense of mastery; they don't need more unnecessary blows from the one place they hoped would be a constant source of feeling in control.

If the master actually gets impaired enough that their behavior is seriously impacting the Team's functioning, it can be a terrifying situation for a vulnerable slave. It's not uncommon for the slave's first reaction to be an abandonment of their submissive role – after all, who wants to be submissive when you don't feel safe? – and a possibly bossy attempt to force the master back onto the path that the slave considers correct, or at least more safe. This is often the worst possible option, because masters tend to be stubborn people who don't take well to being told what to do, and having one's slave suddenly get up in one's face – fueled by all the terror of their own vulnerability – and start making demands feels castrating, regardless of the gender of the master. While some masters will fold and back down, others will snarl back and continue on their path out of principle, even if it's destructive.

While we've seen the in-your-face approach work in some cases, we recommend it only for situations where the master has previously delineated that behavior as an order for the slave – "If my blood sugar crashes, I'm not going to be rational, and I need you to get in my face and argue me down until I eat. I know that I'm going to give you shit about it, but understand that whatever you say to me in that moment, I won't hold it against you when I come out of it, because you'll only be following orders." This approach gives the slave the Nuremburg excuse, and means that they are never fully leaving the dynamic, as opposed to a terrified rebellion in the heat of the moment.

If the master doesn't like that idea – if, for example, they know themselves well and they know that an in-your-face approach will just make things worse, then something different needs to be set in place. We recommend that when panic sets in for the slave, they should lead with a display of both fear and abject surrender. The slave could throw themselves at their master's feet and communicate the following facts:

A) that the slave is still completely subject to the master, and is aware of that fact;

B) that the slave has no right or recourse to make the master act differently, and will go along if there is no other choice;

C) that the master's behavior is absolutely terrifying the slave and making them feel unsafe.

Showing the master their honest, unashamed fear rather than anger or accusation is the best method here. It's a rare master who can see their slave helpless, abject, and extremely distressed through actions that were not intended to distress them (we aren't talking about an SM scene here), and not be immediately moved to do something about it. When my slave is in that space, I want to fix the problem – because I care, because his pain and vulnerability moves me, because it's my job and my honor and my pride as a master and I want to do right by him. I've found that this approach works excellently to push me past whatever fugue I've fallen into, and doesn't set off my "challenge" alarm. And, frankly, if the master is impaired enough that this display doesn't move them to get back in the saddle and start leading the Team in a search for solutions, it's too late and the slave needs to bring in outside help. (We suggest discussing what sort of help to bring in, while you're hopefully doing all this pre-planning – and let me just say that a master with a potential impairment who isolates and refuses an emergency backup system is a disaster waiting to happen to their hapless slave.)

In any case, masters need to remember that slaves can adapt to all sorts of situations, but the one they have the hardest time with is the situation where they don't know what is expected of them. If a master is likely to have (even small) periods of time when they oughtn't to do any mental heavy lifting, and may not even be able to evince much active dominance, the slave needs to be given protocols to get them through that period. The slave needs to know how to tell when such a period has arrived, exactly what is expected of their behavior toward the master, and how to handle external matters which might otherwise have been actively controlled for them. They need to feel the control of the master's standing orders close around them at all times, even when the master isn't able to give that control directly in the moment.

One of the important issues to discuss is what to do if someone's impairment causes them to go drastically wrong. While all parties involved might want to believe that this would never happen, it is worth making up a worst-case plan. If nothing else, unfamiliar medications can occasionally cause unexpected instability and poor thinking. Ideally, if there is a mental health professional involved, they should be informed of these decisions well before they are ever necessary, and be willing to listen to the caveat: "This is what I know right now, while I'm in my right mind, will be best to do. If I'm not in my right mind and I start spouting anything to the contrary, I want that ignored, and this direction followed anyway."

If the couple in question has a therapist or other doctor who is understanding of and friendly toward their power dynamic, they may be able to offer useful information before and during any problematic times. However, each M/s pair needs to decide for themselves how to use their particular dynamic as an exoskeleton – something that not only need not be abandoned when the worst happens, but can carry both parties safely through to the end.

Study Questions

1. What are the slave's impairments? Physical, mental, emotional?
2. What coping mechanisms has the slave used in the past? Do these work well for their role within the power dynamic?
3. If the answer is "...not so well!" can the Team look into finding new coping mechanisms that are just as effective, but don't disrupt the power dynamic?
4. What is the slave's attitude toward their body? If the answer is "...not so good!" how does that affect their ability to self-assess and pass on that information accurately?
5. If the master owns their body, how did that ownership change their attitude? How did it change how they handle their impairments?
6. What are the master's impairments? Physical, mental, emotional?
7. What coping mechanisms is the master used to implementing?
8. How does the slave feel when those coping mechanisms are used? If the answer is "...not so good!" should the Team's efforts in this instance go toward helping the slave to feel better about them, or changing the master's behavior?
9. How can the slave's efforts be best put to helping the master make improvements in handling their impairments?

Part 6:
Team Jobs

Roles and Archetypes

Part of the master's job on the Team is to set the long-term goals for the slave and for the relationship, make the ideal future clear to the slave ("...You'll be able to easily do X, Y, and Z..."), and continually evaluate the actions of both parties as to how they are working toward those goals. Sometimes that means making hard decisions about whether certain aspects need to be triaged or back-burnered. It also means figuring out what roles each person will have, beyond simply The One In Charge and The One Who Follows Orders.

In porn, slaves are generally only seen as performing unskilled labor, or jobs that the master could do better than they could, if the master wanted to bother. This modern portrayal is very different from the ancient Roman model, where supremely competent slaves took the highest prices on the block. Some sociologists and historians have speculated that this came about in America with the widespread institution of racial slavery, where it was deemed important to justify the practice of slavery through "proving" that the enslaved peoples were fundamentally biologically inferior to their masters. Because of this, slaves of more recent periods were often portrayed as being dumb beasts, only good for menial labor.

However, modern consensual slaves may be extremely skilled people with a lot of talents to put at their master's disposal. It's up to the master to figure out how to best utilize the resource that is their human property. Some examples of team roles might be:

✦ **Senior partner/junior partner.** Both people have the same job and the same skills, but differing levels of ability, with the master in the lead. In some cases the slave even has higher levels of ability, but the master makes the final decision, perhaps from a full spectrum of information given by the slave.

✦ **Mentor/apprentice.** This is like the above pattern, but there is active learning going on, and the ideal is for the subordinate partner to eventually become as skilled as the lead partner, and possibly surpass them.

✦ **Assistant.** The slave has a job as support staff that may consist of an entirely different set of skills from that of the master. As many personal assistants can tell you, assisting someone smoothly and competently is very different from taking the lead position. It may require skills that the lead person doesn't have, and wouldn't be good at.

✦ **Separate spheres.** Each has different jobs which don't interfere with each other, nor overlap in more than a perfunctory way. "Traditional" gendered marriage roles follow this pattern, with the wife ruling household matters and the husband working outside the home and/or fixing things around the house. The difficulty with this set of roles is that the person in charge needs to get very good information from their partner in order to make larger decisions, or else they need to decide to step back and trust the subordinate partner entirely.

Gender Roles

It's nearly impossible to talk about master/slave relationship roles without bringing up the thorny problem of gender. We've seen it asked of slaves on various online lists and forums: What are the most challenging things (outside of sex) that your master or mistress has asked you to do? The overwhelming majority of answers, we noted with amusement, reflected some activity that was contrary to the slave's concept of what someone of their gender ought to be doing. This was especially a problem for female slaves, many of whom had romanticized or even eroticized stereotypical cultural female roles as part of their subservient preference. Being stereotypically female in all the ways that promote helplessness, or at least limit competence to the domestic sphere, was tied both to their sense of being a slave and their sense of being female. When a (usually male) master decided that there was no reason for him to do yardwork or put up that shelf, being that he had a perfectly good slave who was supposed to do whatever he said, these female slaves bridled and felt threatened. You can imagine what happened when he went further and decided that he didn't want to pay for an oil change, and his slave was going to learn how to do that.

Some slaves of any gender, of course, are fine with doing whatever needs to be done so long as it is within their skillset, or they can manage to learn. It is also true that some female slaves come to M/s with a good deal of discomfort regarding stereotypical female roles (perhaps except during sex), and are disheartened by masters who demand that they give up jeans and wear dresses and makeup. For every female slave who whines about being made to do "unfeminine" work like changing a flat tire (or fucking someone with a strap-on), there is one who hesitantly discusses her ambivalence with the rigid gender presentation demanded by her male master. When heterosexual male masters "feminize" their not-so-feminine slaves, it is usually because they have also eroticized the conflation of stereotypical female gender roles with submission. (But more on that in a moment.)

Male slaves, in general, while not thrilled with learning to give manicures or (insert other feminine activity), tend to come to slavery with an understanding that to be a male slave is to buck the stereotypical status quo anyway, so they may expect to have little recourse with regard to types of chores. Some of them eroticize traditionally "feminine" chores as a form of degradation, which we find a bit problematic – all service should be seen, ideally, as valuable if the master wants it – but it may be what gets them through the day until they get used to the idea and it becomes just another thing to do.

There are many reasons why a master might order a socially conventional slave to do activities that are outside of their gender-role comfort zone. One might be, as we've mentioned above, that the job just needs to get done, and the master's only got one slave, and so it's their job. Another reason might be pleasure – a more sadistic master might honestly enjoy the discomfort of their slave struggling with a role that they were told wasn't right for them to enact. However, a third reason might be to make a point that the master has the right to alter any part of the slave's visible identity. It can be a way of breaking through cultural conditioning on a very deep-seated issue, paving the way for the master to break through other cultural assumptions. In a way, it can be the master saying, "I don't bottom to cultural assumptions. I may choose to follow them or not as I decide, and I'm certainly not going to bottom to the people who taught you that gender should be enacted in a certain way. If I own you, I own your external identity as well – and I can make alterations to it as I choose." This point may be less strongly hammered home over chores and more so over external appearances.

When the problem isn't that the slave has specific ideas about their conventional gender role, but that the slave has spent their life deliberately avoiding the trappings of their assigned gender role – and perhaps actively going against them – and the master would like to herd them back into a more conventional role and appearance, the situation needs to be approached more gently and mindfully. In some cases, the slave in question has spent years assessing and rejecting gender roles; this may not be as much a kneejerk reaction as a thoughtful refutation based on personal or political beliefs. If the master comes to the situation with "I want to make you look like a 'normal' member of X gender," this may be met with resistance if the slave is well aware of many forms of gender expression, and why it's fair to say that there is no "normal". It works better – and is more honest – for the master to say, "I prefer to see my s-type with this kind of gender expression, so you're going to do that for me."

One such M/s pair that we know has a male dominant and a female slave who doesn't consider herself exactly female – instead, she feels that she is somewhat androgynous and slightly genderqueer. Her master prefers that she appear more traditionally feminine, because that's what he finds attractive. They've managed to make this work because his attitude is basically, "Yes, I know it doesn't come natural to you; I know it's an act. But it's an act that I believe you can accomplish for my pleasure."

It's important, in these cases, for the master to acknowledge and appreciate who the slave is at their core, and have at least a small place where they can express that identity. This is especially true if the slave has fought years of shame over not having a socially conventional gender expression. "I spent years being ashamed of being a sissy, and feeling bad that I couldn't make it work to be a macho guy, and now you're telling me that you want me to dress like a macho guy? Are you ashamed of me?" is best countered with, "I know you're a sissy, and I am fine with that. But I'd like you to butch it up sometimes because I find it hot."

It's important for the master to figure out the roots of the objection to traditional gender presentation, because that will determine the best approach. For example, if a given female-bodied slave bridles at wearing dresses, is this because:

A) She suffers from low self-esteem about her appearance and doesn't believe that she will ever be an attractive woman, and so she dresses in a schlumpy, androgynous way.

B) She is dorky and awkward, and is afraid that if she tries to dress in a conventionally feminine way, she'll get it wrong and look stupid, although she might not be opposed to it if she was trained to do it correctly.

C) She was taught that women who dress like that are weak and submissive, and that it's degrading, and she is struggling with feeling as if she likes the degrading aspect of it.

D) She was taught that women who dress like that are weak and submissive, and that it's degrading, and she is strongly against it because it would be "letting the side down" or proclaiming that she is weak and worthy of degradation.

E) She identifies as butch, sexually and/or socially, and feels most comfortable and sexy with a masculine gender presentation.

F) She/he is actually a female-to-male transsexual who hasn't dealt with her gender issues yet, and when she/he does so, she/he will probably want to get sex reassignment.

Obviously, this is a wide range of motivations, and some of them will be far more damaging to force into a more socially conventional gender expression. While slaves A and B might find a great sexual and self-worth awakening in the Cinderella treatment, slaves C and D would require a great deal more special handling to get there, and E and F would probably be traumatized – or be forced to find a different dominant. Similarly, there's a very different slant to butching up an effeminate male slave who acts like a sissy because he's absorbed propaganda about how all male slaves have to be weak and effeminate (or alternately, because being a sissy maid is a sexual fetish of his and he hasn't developed an understanding of himself as a slave outside of sexual fetishes), and trying to do it to that slender vision in black lace who's been to drag bars for years and spent ages getting his eyeliner just right.

For the record, a master has the right to order the gender-role-ambivalent slave to apply themselves to figuring out why they hold a certain attitude about their looks, and present a brutally honest report to the master. If the master doesn't have every part of that information, they might inadvertently misstep in a way that might lose that slave. For that matter, if there are strong deal-breakers that might come up on either side, it's best to get that over with as early as possible in the dating process.

One way for a master to tell if a potential slave is unsure of culturally-acceptable appearances due to issues or attractiveness, self-esteem, or flat-out gender identity that is significantly further along the gender spectrum is to ask them to meet the master somewhere, dressed up as nicely as possible in clothing that makes the slave feel attractive and sexy. Make sure to reinforce that it should be entirely the slave's choice, and not what the slave believes the master might want. If the slave keeps trying to mentally track back to the master's preferences, the master needs to remind them, "My preference is to examine your preference." Slaves who have trouble finding anything that makes them feel sexy and attractive without someone else's validation need to be sent back to the drawing board to study themselves and their motivations, and report back. However, if she shows up dressed to the nines as a dapper butch, or he shows up with multiple earrings and a sultry off-the-shoulder belly shirt, it's clear that these are slaves who should have masters who have a strong appreciation for that type. While some of them might adapt to a more conventional role with a lot of effort (and probably only if everything else in the relationship was nearly perfect), it might be kinder and easier for them to find a better match.

Study Questions

1. What roles do you have as part of the Team?
2. What archetypes inspire you personally, separately and together? What archetypes do you see in your partner, and would they agree with this image?
3. What gendered patterns do you each bring into this relationship?
4. What gendered patterns have you built, rebuilt, or dismantled as part of this relationship?
5. Are there parts of those patterns that you feel might unnecessarily limit your ability to be effective in the relationship? Are there parts that enhance it? Are there parts that do both?
6. How do societal patterns, or your upbringing, affect how you express gender in this relationship?
7. What direct control does the master take over the slave's gender expression? What subtle effects do their wishes have over the slave's gender expression?
8. What control does the slave's expectations have over the master's gender expression?

About the Authors

Raven Kaldera is a queer FTM transgendered intersexual shaman. He is the author of too many books to list here, including *Dark Moon Rising: Pagan BDSM And The Ordeal Path* and *Power Circuits: Polyamory In A Power Dynamic*. He and his slaveboy Joshua have been teaching and presenting workshops regularly for many years to the BDSM, Neo-Pagan, Sex/Spirituality, transgender, and other communities. 'Tis an ill wind that blows no minds.

Joshua Tenpenny is Raven's Boy, and his devoted assistant, partner, and slave for life. He is a massage therapist, Shiatsu practitioner, and yoga teacher. He is polymorphously perverse, and finds spiritual fulfillment through any kind of worthy service. This is the second book he has co-authored with his master, the first being *Dear Raven And Joshua: Questions And Answers About Master/Slave Relationships*.

* 9 7 8 0 9 8 2 8 7 9 4 6 7 *